Hangin' With BRITNEY

By
Anne Cadman

Scholastic Inc.

New York   Toronto London   Auckland   Sydney
Mexico City   New Delhi   Hong Kong   Buenos Aires

Photo Credits:

Front cover: London Features; page 1: Paul Fenton/Shooting Star; page 3: Barry Talesnick/Retna LTD; page 4: Peter Hitchison/Retna LTD; page 5: Larry Busacca/Retna LTD; page 6: Ernie Paniccoli (middle left); Retna LTD (middle right); page 7: Jon James/London Features (bottom left); E. Catarina (middle right); pages 8-9: All from Jared Poppell/Classmates.com Yearbook Archive; page 10: Ron Wolfson/London Features; page 11: All Action/Retna; page 12: D. Charriau/Retna (bottom left); Gie Knaeps/London Features (bottom right); page 13: Tara Canova/Retna LTD (top left); Melvin Jones/London Features(top right); pages 14-15: Bill Davila/Retna LTD; page 16: Sam Levi/Retna LTD; page 17: Gregg Deguire/ London Features; page 18: Ron Wolfson/London Features (left); Paul Smith/Retna LTD (right); page 19: Ron Wolfson/London Features (top left); Joseph Marzullo Retna LTD (bottom middle); Jon Furniss/All Action/Retna (top right); page 20: David Atlas/Retna LTD; page 21: Ron Wolfson/London Features (top right /bottom right/top left); Kevin Mazur/London Features (bottom left); page 22: Steve Granitz/Retna LTD (top left); T. Bone Smith/Retna LTD (bottom right); page 23: Steve Granitz/Retna LTD; page 24: Peter Hitchison All Action/Retna.

This book is unaffiliated with and not sponsored by Britney Spears.

ISBN 0-439-33039-4

Published by Scholastic Inc. All rights reserved.

SCHOLASTIC and associated logos are trademarks and/ or registered trademarks of Scholastic Inc.

12 11 10 9 8 7 6 5 4 3 2 1   1 2 3 4 5 6/0

Printed in the U.S.A.
First Scholastic printing, October 2001

CONTENTS

Here's Britney!

Who hasn't heard of Britney Spears?! She sings and she dances and she's got fans across the globe. But way back when, the little girl with the sweet voice never thought that she'd be as mega-famous as she is today. She was actually a shy child who enjoyed playing with her dolls. But as she grew older, she knew that she wanted to shine like a star more than anything.

A Star Is Born

Britney was born in Kentwood, Louisiana, on December 2, 1981. Kentwood is a very small town — only about 1,200 people live there. Believe it or not, Britney's first words were song lyrics. She says the radio taught her to sing because she would hear a song and learn it lickety-split.

Britney is still just a regular girl at heart.

Full of Energy

The pop princess-in-training loved to dance around her living room when she was little. She had so much energy that, once she was old enough, she started taking gymnastics, ballet, and tap-dancing classes. All the awards bitty Britney won were a sign of the times to come, that's for sure!

Famous at Home

Britney loves the moments when she can put on a pair of jeans and just relax.

Britney gave her first "performance" at her kindergarten graduation. She sang "What Child Is This." By the time Britney was ten years old she was already a celebrity to the people of her town. She had moved to New York City and acted in a play called *Ruthless* in which she played a mean little girl. (You know she's a great actress if she could pull off acting nasty!) And, she had appeared on the weekly TV talent show, *Star Search*. Britney won the first round but lost the second. Good thing she didn't let that setback halt her dreams!

Cast at Last

When Britney was eleven, she joined the cast of a TV show called the *New Mickey Mouse Club*. She made lots of friends, since the cast was made up entirely of kids. Some of her costars were named Justin Timberlake, JC Chasez, and Christina Aguilera. (Of course, none of them were big-time stars yet.) Britney loved being on the show because she could showcase her singing and dancing — two things she did very well.

Britney had a dream, and it came true!

Home Again

When *MMC* went off the air, Britney went back home to Kentwood. She liked being "a regular kid" again. But after a while, she got that itch again. "I wasn't happy just hanging around at home. I wanted to see the world and make music," she said.

On Her Own

Hmmm, how could Britney make her dream of being a singer come true? Well, she thought and thought and came up with an idea. She'd make a tape of herself singing and send it to a record company. That's exactly what she did, and guess what? They called her to come to New York City and sing for them in person! Jive Records fell in love with Britney and her voice, and they signed her up to make an album.

Making a CD

Britney flew across the ocean to Sweden where she recorded her very first CD. It had eleven songs on it. One was written by Britney herself! (It's called "I'm So Curious.") Soon, " . . . Baby One More Time" was on the radio and Britney's star began to rise.

Being a star takes you all over the world. Here's Britney very far away from home in Paris, France.

Did someone say shop?! Britney's fave thing to do besides sing is shop!

Everyone Knows Her Name

These days, Britney has traveled all over the world performing her songs. She's made many videos and she's even sung at the Super Bowl. Millions of fans adore her. She reached her goal — to sing and dance and have everyone know her name!

BRITNEY'S SCHOOL DAYS

First Grade

Second Grade

Third Grade

Fourth Grade

Sixth Grade

Britney always liked to smile for the camera, even when she was just in school!

Seventh Grade

Britney was a Homecoming Maid at Parklane Academy.

Eighth Grade

fast facts

Britney's favorite subject in school was English. Her least favorite was geometry.

did you know

Britney's nickname when she was little was Bit-Bit!

Britney made her varsity basketball team.

CHAPTER 3

BRITNEY BEST

how well do you know Britney? Take a look and see!

FULL NAME: Britney Jean Spears

NICKNAME: Brit

BIRTHDAY: December 2, 1981

BIRTHPLACE: Kentwood, Louisiana

HAIR COLOR: Blond

EYE COLOR: Brown

PARENTS' NAMES: Lynne and Jamie Spears

SISTER'S NAME: Jamie Lynn

BROTHER'S NAME: Bryan

HEIGHT: 5 feet, 4 inches

FAVORITE ACTORS: Ben Affleck, Brad Pitt

FAVORITE ACTRESS: Jennifer Aniston

FAVORITE AUTHOR: Danielle Steel

FAVORITE DRINK: Iced coffee drinks

Britney's first car was a white Mercedes, just like the one you see here.

Britney loves to collect dolls. She has a bunch of Britney Spears dolls in her collection, of course!

FAVORITE SPORTS: Gymnastics and basketball

FAVORITE SINGER: Whitney Houston

PETS: A dog named Bitzi (but Britney calls her Baby)

WHAT MAKES HER FEEL GOOD: Shopping and reading

SHE LIKES TO COLLECT: Dolls and fairies

WORST HABIT: Biting her nails

FAVORITE FOODS: Pasta, grilled chicken, hot dogs

FAVORITE COLOR: Baby blue

FAVORITE HAT: Baseball cap

FAVORITE ICE-CREAM FLAVOR: Chocolate chip cookie dough

FAVORITE CEREAL: Cocoa Puffs

CHAPTER 4 PERFORMING!

There are a lot of things that Britney has to do before she can go onstage. She has to:

1 Put on makeup. It might look like Britney is wearing a lot of makeup, but that's because when she's onstage, she wants to make sure that everyone in the audience can see her face. She has a makeup artist help apply the colors to her eyes, her lips, and her cheeks.

2 Put on costumes. One of the best parts of watching Britney perform is looking at the different clothes she wears. She needs someone to help her pick out the clothes and help her change into them. Sometimes she wears as many as seven different outfits in one night.

"The thing I like most about my outfits is that they're fun and they're young."

No matter what Britney wears, she always looks great when she performs.

Though she's sung all around the world, Britney loves when she gets back to Disney World in Florida. She used to film the *New Mickey Mouse Club* there.

3 Fix her hair. Britney has worn her hair long, short, and even in ponytails. A hair stylist makes sure that she always looks her best.

4 Warm-up. Britney does throat exercises to make sure her voice is ready for a night of singing. She also stretches to make sure that she can dance without getting hurt.

5 Remember her dance steps. When Britney sings, she has to dance at the same time. That's not always easy to do!

BRITNEY'S fans!

Britney loves her fans. She knows that she wouldn't be a big star without them. If you ever run into Britney, don't feel shy about walking up to her and saying hello. She would probably greet you and your friends with a big smile and say, "How y'all doing?" Why would Britney be so nice? Here's a secret: Britney still gets excited when *she* meets famous people!

"The best feeling in the world is when I'm singing and the audience is singing the words along with me."

a very expensive pair of jeans!

Britney and several other stars donated their old blue jeans for an Internet auction to raise money for the National Multiple Sclerosis Society. Britney's jeans had been designed just for her, so they were really special to her. And she autographed them for the auction. One fan wanted the jeans so much that he paid $7,020 for them!

"I love giving out autographs when people recognize me."

The Joy of Britney

"I want to thank my fans so much for supporting me."

Were you glued to your TV set when you first saw Britney's Pepsi commercial? If you haven't seen it, it's like a mini-movie where Britney is singing and dancing in a Pepsi factory and on a rooftop. It also shows her fans watching the commercial, and even trying to imitate Britney's moves. The whole thing took three days to film, and even though Britney's costume was simple — a pair of blue jeans and a white halter top — she still had to spend two hours getting her hair and makeup to look just right for the camera. But that didn't stop her from doing what she loves when she had some downtime on the set. She played basketball and she didn't worry about getting sweaty and messing up her style!

Write Britney a Fan Letter

If you're a big Britney fan, tell her so! Sit down and write her a fan letter. (She says she tries to answer as many letters as she can.) If you don't know what to write don't worry, here's help: Tell her why you like her music. Tell her which of her costumes you like the best. Or just tell her something about yourself that would make her smile, like you put on shows for your family pretending you're Britney Spears! You can send your letter to:

Britney Spears Fan Club
P.O. Box 192730
San Francisco, CA, 94119

Or you can visit her Web site at www.britneyspears.com

CHAPTER 6

BRITNEY'S MAMA!

Britney's best friend is her mother, Lynne. The two are so close that Britney can't wait to come home to Kentwood to see her. "You just get that feeling when you're there, just a warm feeling inside. That's all that matters," she says. Britney bought a new house in her hometown so that her family would have more space. She even treated her mom to a car (a shiny black Porsche) so that she could get around town in style.

One of the reasons that Britney likes coming home is so that she can sleep in her own bed and eat her mother's cooking. "My mom is the best cook in the world," she says. And Lynne knows that when Britney comes to Kentwood, she has to make her daughter's favorite dish — chicken and dumplings.

Britney has lots of clothes, shoes, and jewelry, but the one thing that she loves the most is a ring her mother gave her. She wears it on her pinky finger. Her mom gave the same ring to her sister, Jamie, and her brother, Bryan.

Britney likes to work with her mother whenever she can. (No, her mom doesn't sing and dance with her!) Lynne taught her daughter how to read when she was little. Now, Britney shares her mother's love for books. So Britney and Lynne wrote a book together! It's called *Britney Spears' Heart to Heart*, and it tells the story of Britney and Lynne's closeness. They also wrote a novel called *A Mother's Gift* about a small-town girl who hits it big. (Britney and Lynne know all about that!)

Britney's on display in a museum!

Britney and her mother love to laugh together. Britney isn't embarrassed to say Mom is her best friend and she tells her all her troubles.

The Kentwood Museum in Britney's hometown is adding a collection of Britney's things so that her fans can get to know her even better. The collection is in three sections: early childhood, the *New Mickey Mouse Club* years, and Britney as a star. Britney's parents have given the museum some personal items from Britney's closet, such as dresses she used to wear, which will be on display. Some of Brit's more memorable duds were pretty, um, far-out! "I had plaid skirts, cowboy boots, a homemade hat with rhinestones on it and a little tie!" The Kentwood Museum is right near the Louisiana-Mississippi border, so if you're ever in the area, add it to your list of must-see places!

AWaRDS!

Britney has had to learn to give acceptance speeches because she's won so many awards! On this special night in 1999, she won four *Billboard* Music Awards, for Female Artist of the Year, Female Hot 100 Singles Artist of the Year, Female Album Artist of the Year, and New Artist of the Year.

Britney has won tons of awards. And winning is cool, but getting dressed up is fun, too! For some awards shows, Brit goes glamorous and for others she gets funky. But she always looks beautiful!

More trophies! Britney is thrilled to have them!

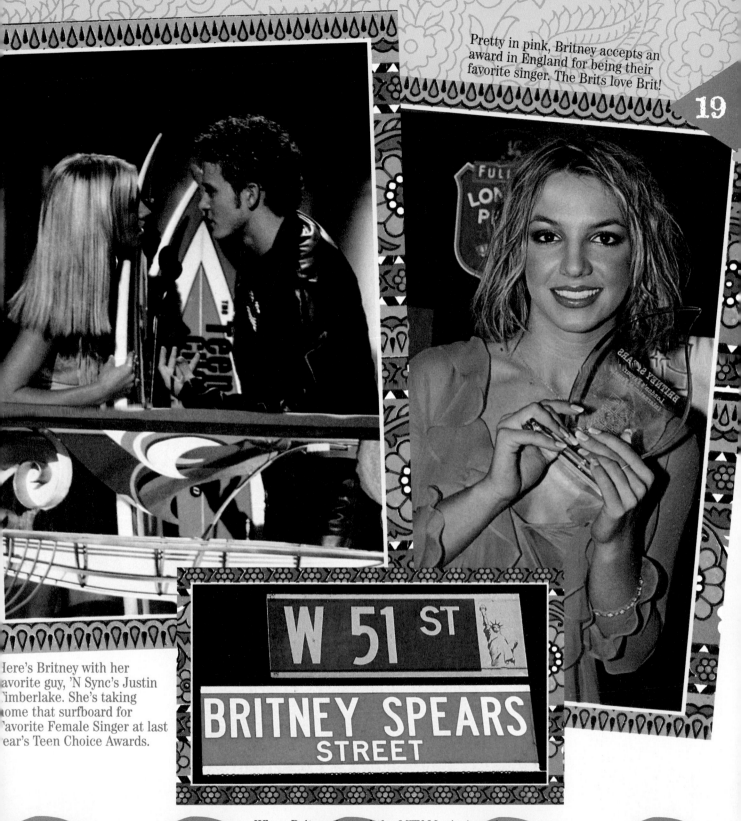

Pretty in pink, Britney accepts an award in England for being their favorite singer. The Brits love Brit!

Here's Britney with her favorite guy, 'N Sync's Justin Timberlake. She's taking home that surfboard for favorite Female Singer at last year's Teen Choice Awards.

W 51 ST
BRITNEY SPEARS STREET

When Britney hosted the MTV Music Awards in New York City, the mayor changed one of the street signs for the evening in her honor.

Celebrities love hanging out with other celebrities. See which stars Britney hangs with!

Jessica Simpson runs over to tell her friend Britney a secret at the Teen Choice Awards.

Britney met Melissa Joan Hart when she guest starred on *Sabrina the Teenage Witch*. The girls got along so well that Britney had Melissa appear in her "(You Drive Me) Crazy" video.

Ed McMahon was the host of *Star Search* when Britney appeared on it all those years ago. When they met up again recently, they got along like old friends.

Justin Timberlake and Britney have known each other since they both appeared on the *New Mickey Mouse Club* together. Britney opened for 'N Sync on their tour a few years ago. Don't she and Justin make a cute couple?

DID YOU KNOW?

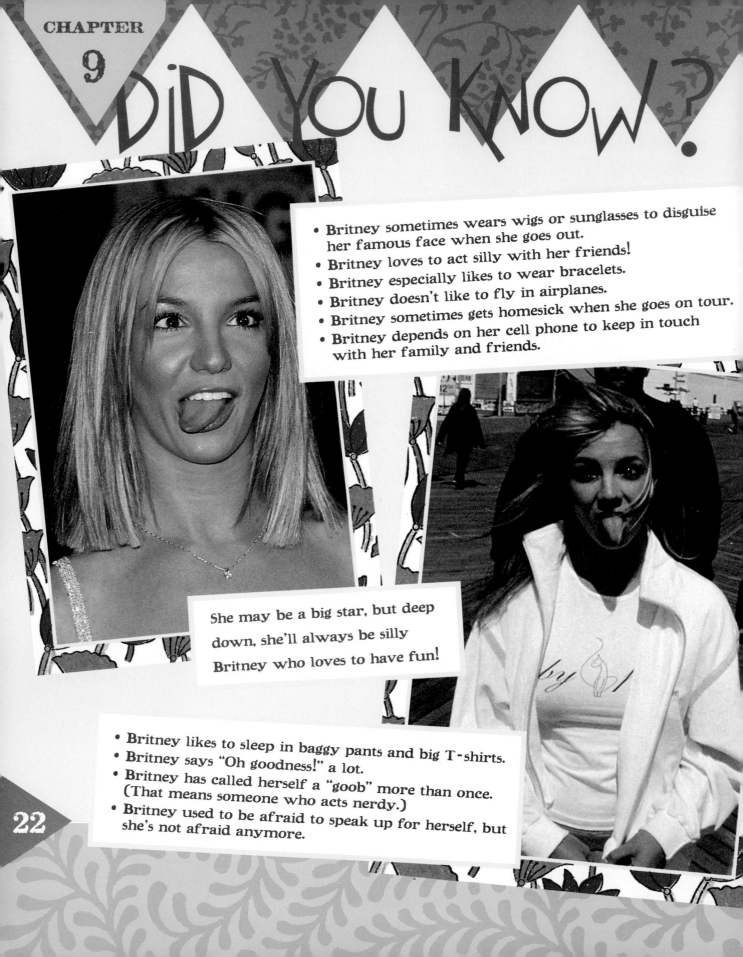

- Britney sometimes wears wigs or sunglasses to disguise her famous face when she goes out.
- Britney loves to act silly with her friends!
- Britney especially likes to wear bracelets.
- Britney doesn't like to fly in airplanes.
- Britney sometimes gets homesick when she goes on tour.
- Britney depends on her cell phone to keep in touch with her family and friends.

She may be a big star, but deep down, she'll always be silly Britney who loves to have fun!

- Britney likes to sleep in baggy pants and big T-shirts.
- Britney says "Oh goodness!" a lot.
- Britney has called herself a "goob" more than once. (That means someone who acts nerdy.)
- Britney used to be afraid to speak up for herself, but she's not afraid anymore.

22

Singing will always be Britney's first love, but she also loves to try something new. Like a movie! No, she's not giving up singing, but she has said for a long time that she really wants to try out acting again. Her days as a Mouseketeer gave Brit a taste of acting, and she thought it was so yummy that she wants to taste it again! The movie *What Friends Are For*, which Brit was slated to film this past spring, is about a young singer who travels to Los Angeles, California, with her friends to enter a talent competition. And who do you think plays the singer? Britney, of course!

Britney takes her career very seriously . . .

Certain sounds will always make you think of fall — like the sound of leaves being raked and school buses arriving. Add Britney's new album to the list of sounds that will always make you think of this time of year. Her third disk was scheduled to drop in late summer or early fall. On it, Britney reinvents herself once again, but what stays the same is her fantastic voice! She plays a few guitar licks in some songs, so listen up for that!

. . . but she also likes to get goofy!

Britney's a PlayStation 2 game! Back in the spring of 2001, Britney was being worked up to become a virtual hero on a new video game title. It'll be Britney like you've never seen her before!

Hangin' with 'N sync

By Anne Cadman

Scholastic Inc.

New York   Toronto   London   Auckland   Sydney
Mexico City   New Delhi   Hong Kong   Buenos Aires

Photo Credits:

Front Cover: Ilpo Musto/London Features; page 4: Tara Canova/Retna LTD (top left); David Atlas/Retna LTD (middle); Joseph Galea (bottom right); page 5: Bill Davila/Retna LTD (top left); David Atlas/Retna LTD; (middle) Ron Wolfson/London Features (bottom right); page 6: David Atlas/Retna LTD (top left); Bill Davila/Retna LTD (middle left); Bernhard Kuhmsted/Retna LTD (middle right); Roba Press/Shooting Star (bottom right); page 7: Dennis Van Tine/London Features (top right); Ron Wolfson/London Features (top left); Joseph Galea (middle left); Steve Jennings/Retna LTD (middle right); Ron Wolfson/London Features (bottom left); Eric Antanitus/Retna LTD (bottom right); page 8: Steve Granitz/Retna LTD (top left); Ron Wolfson/London Features (bottom right); page 9: David Atlas/Retna LTD; page 10: Steve Granitz/Retna LTD (top left); page 11: Bill Davila/Retna LTD (bottom left); Steve Granitz/Retna LTD (top right); pages: 12-13: Jared Poppel Classmates.com Yearbook Archives; page 14: ULM/London Features; page 15: David Atlas/Retna LTD (top right); Mark Shenley/Retna LTD (bottom); page 16: Henny Garfunkel/Retna LTD; page 17: Paul Smith Retna LTD (bottom left); Eric Antanitus/Retna LTD (top right); pages 18-19: Jared Poppel Classmates.com Yearbook Archives; page 20: Tammie Arroyo/Retna Ltd; page 21: David Atlas/Retna LTD (top); Ed Geller/ Retna LTD (bottom); page 22: Steve Granitz/Retna LTD (middle); Bill Davila/Retna LTD (bottom right); page 23: Mary Monaco (Shooting Star); (top) Bill Davila/Retna LTD; page 24: Ron Wolfson/London Features.

This book is unaffiliated with and not sponsored by 'N Sync.

ISBN 0-439-33039-4

Published by Scholastic Inc. All rights reserved.

SCHOLASTIC and associated logos are trademarks and/ or registered trademarks of Scholastic Inc.

12 11 10 9 8 7 6 5 4 3 2 1   1 2 3 4 5 6/0

Printed in the U.S.A.
First Scholastic printing, October 2001

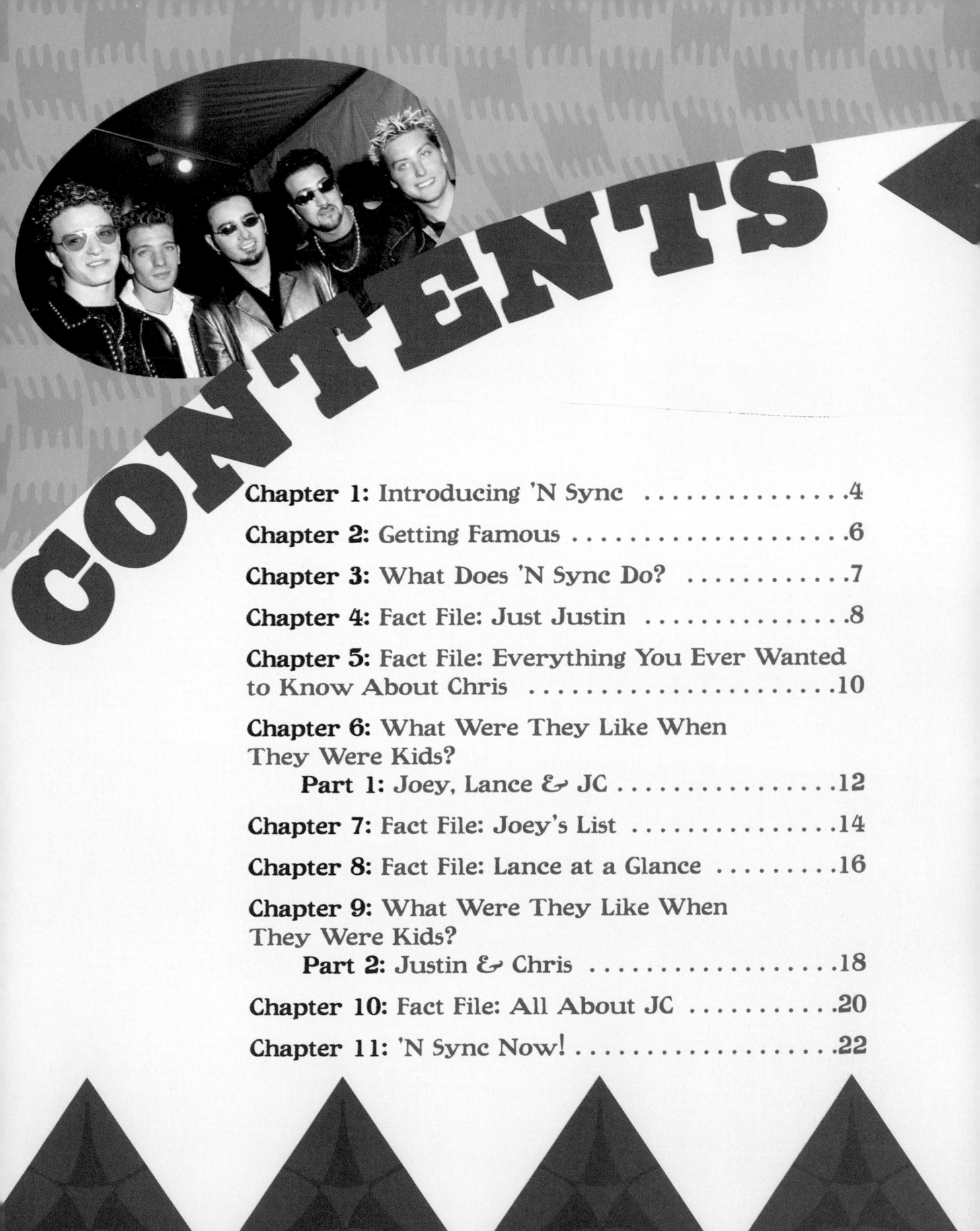

CONTENTS

CHAPTER 1

INTRODUCING 'N SYNC

'N Sync is everywhere! Their songs are on the radio. Their videos are on TV. Their faces are on magazine covers all over the world. They've made their fans everywhere smile. In one word, they've become famous. How did Justin Timberlake, JC Chasez, Joey Fatone, Lance Bass, and Chris Kirkpatrick go from being regular kids to superstars? Well, it wasn't easy. But they set a goal for themselves and they never gave up.

How Did It All Begin?

Justin Timberlake and JC Chasez met each other on the set of a TV show called the *New Mickey Mouse Club.* Hundreds of kids from all over the United States who could sing, dance, and act tried out for a spot on the show. Justin joined the cast when he was eleven years old and JC when he was sixteen. You might think that because JC was a whole five years older than Justin they wouldn't have had a lot in common, but that wasn't true. In fact, they became fast friends because both boys had a huge interest in music.

JUSTIN

JC

JC on the *New Mickey Mouse Club.*

JOEY

Meanwhile...

Joey Fatone and Chris Kirkpatrick had jobs at Universal Studios in Orlando, Florida. Chris was in a group called the Hollywood HiTones and Joey was the Wolfman in the Beetlejuice Graveyard Review. Joey and Chris liked to hang out together when they weren't working.

When Chris knew he was ready for bigger things, he decided to put together a singing group of his own. Joey said he was in. Chris remembered a talented kid named Justin whom he had met on different auditions in Orlando. Justin loved the idea of being in a group, and he called his <u>MMC</u> pal JC to see if he was interested. Joey, Chris, JC, and Justin sang together and they thought that they had a great sound. But they all agreed that something was still missing.

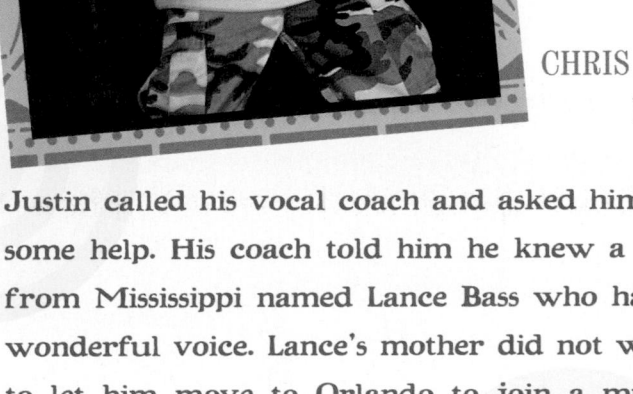

CHRIS

TWO LANCES!

Justin called his vocal coach and asked him for some help. His coach told him he knew a teen from Mississippi named Lance Bass who had a wonderful voice. Lance's mother did not want to let him move to Orlando to join a music group — at first. But Lance did a bunch of begging and Mrs. Bass finally agreed to let her son go. 'N Sync was born!

Lance: "We clicked instantly. The first thing we sang together was 'The Star-Spangled Banner.'"

GETTING FAMOUS

'N Sync had a lot of hard work ahead of them. They had to learn a bunch of new things before they could become superstars. Like what?

1 **Learn to dance together.** At first, this was very hard for Lance, who admits dancing's not his greatest strength. But he's a great dancer now!

2 **Learn to sing together.** Each member of 'N Sync has a beautiful voice, but if anyone were to sing off-key it would sound awful! They had to make sure that they sang in tune with one another all the time.

3 **Practice every day.** Singing and dancing at the same time isn't easy. 'N Sync spent many long hours rehearsing in an old warehouse until they felt that they were perfect.

4 **Pick out clothes.** The boys wanted to have a certain "look." They knew they would have to impress people at record companies (and their fans), so they wanted to look their best.

5 **Make a tape/CD of themselves** to send out to record companies. 'N Sync recorded their voices and made a videotape of their act. They had to prove to record companies they had the right stuff!

Then and now — wow, what a difference!

Not too long after 'N Sync did all of those things they were signed to a record deal. This meant that they would record a CD with thirteen songs on it. Their first song, "I Want You Back," would be played on the radio and their CD would be in record stores. It was finally happening for the fantastic five!

This is how 'N Sync looked when they were just starting out.

WHAT DOES 'N SYNC DO?

Lots of things!

They sign copies of their CD for happy fans.

They talk to TV reporters.

'N Sync's newest CD, Celebrity, is packed with groovin' tunes.

They dress in costumes when they perform.

They sing onstage.

They meet their fans.

They meet other stars. (Here's JC with Destiny's Child.)

FACT FILE: JUST JUSTIN

FULL NAME: Justin Randall Timberlake

NICKNAME: Curly

BIRTHDAY: January 31, 1981

BIRTHPLACE: Memphis, Tennessee

HAIR COLOR: Blond

EYE COLOR: Blue

PARENTS' NAMES: Lynn Harless and Randy Timberlake

BROTHERS' NAMES: Randy and Stephen

HEIGHT: 6 feet

FAVORITE ACTORS: Brad Pitt, Samuel L. Jackson

FAVORITE ACTRESSES: Meg Ryan, Sandra Bullock

FAVORITE MOVIE: *Ferris Bueller's Day Off*

FAVORITE DRINK: Milk

FAVORITE SPORT: Basketball

FAVORITE SINGER: Brian McKnight

HERO: Michael Jordan

FAVORITE ANIMAL: Dog

FIRST PET: A dog named Scooter

PETS HE HAS NOW: Two dogs, named Bella and Bearlie

FAVORITE AUTHOR: John Grisham

Did you know that Justin thinks his nose is too big?

WHAT MAKES HIM FEEL GOOD: Exercise

FAVORITE FOOD: Pasta and cereal

FAVORITE CEREAL: Cap'n Crunch, Frosted Flakes, Apple Jacks

FAVORITE CANDY: Sprees

FAVORITE ICE-CREAM FLAVOR: Coffee

FAVORITE COLOR: Baby blue

FAVORITE THING TO BUY: Sneakers

WHAT MAKES HIM BLUSH: Compliments

BIGGEST FEARS: Sharks, snakes

WORST HABIT: Being messy

FIRST CONCERT: The Beach Boys

Not only can Justin sing, he can also play the keyboards and the guitar.

FACT FILE: EVERYTHING YOU EVER WANTED TO KNOW ABOUT CHRIS

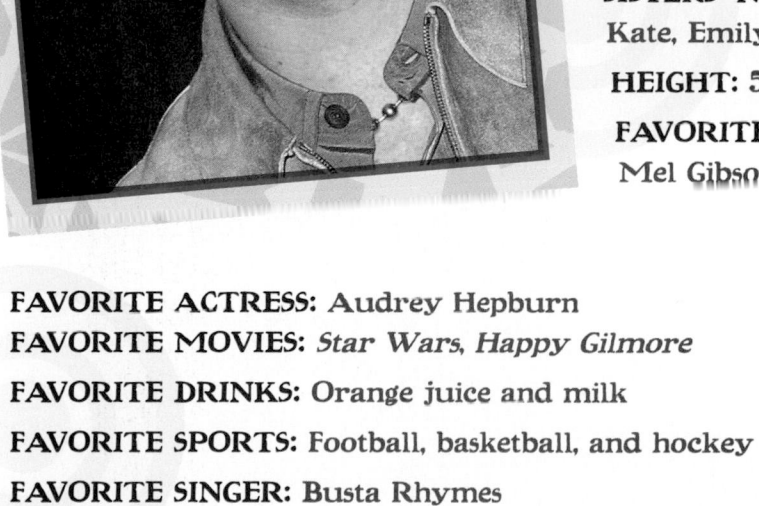

FULL NAME: Christopher Alan Kirkpatrick

NICKNAMES: Lucky, Tricky

BIRTHDAY: October 17, 1971

BIRTHPLACE: Clarion, Pennsylvania

HAIR COLOR: Brown

EYE COLOR: Brown

MOM'S NAME: Beverly Eustice

SISTERS' NAMES: Molly, Kate, Emily, and Taylor

HEIGHT: 5 feet, 9 inches

FAVORITE ACTOR: Mel Gibson

FAVORITE ACTRESS: Audrey Hepburn

FAVORITE MOVIES: *Star Wars, Happy Gilmore*

FAVORITE DRINKS: Orange juice and milk

FAVORITE SPORTS: Football, basketball, and hockey

FAVORITE SINGER: Busta Rhymes

FIRST PET: A dog named Lisa

PETS HE HAS NOW: Two dogs, named Busta and Korea

WHAT MAKES HIM FEEL GOOD: Rollerblading

FAVORITE FOOD: Tacos

FAVORITE COLORS: Silver, black, and red

BIGGEST FEAR: Heights

FIRST CONCERT: Weird Al Yankovic

Chris says that the other members of 'N Sync aren't just his friends — they're more like his brothers.

Chris is always serious about music — but not about much else! Life is fun and games!

When it comes to helping charities, especially any that help kids, Chris is there! He played b-ball to benefit a children's charity last year.

WHAT WERE THEY LIKE WHEN THEY WERE KIDS?

Part 1: Joey, Lance & JC

Truthfully, they were pretty normal. They went to school, they played sports, and they loved getting attention. You might find these photos funny, but don't laugh too hard — everyone has to start somewhere!

Joey wore a uniform — complete with a tie — to his Catholic school, and after school he got comfy in jeans and a tee.

This is Joey's yearbook picture from high school. He says that high school was one of the best times of his life.

One of the things that Joey loves to do is make people laugh. His imitation of Cher (left) in a school play is sure to make *you* laugh!

Joey was always told that he had a great voice. That's because he practiced using it.

This picture was taken during JC's very first year of high school in Bowie, Maryland. JC remembers that when he was little, he liked toy cars. In fact, JC still loves cars today — but now he likes the ones he can drive himself!

Can you believe that Lance's friends and family were convinced he would probably grow up to be a comedian because he was so funny as a kid?

Lance liked playing games when he was younger. Here, he and a classmate tried their best to win the three-legged race during the "Clash of the Classes" at school.

FACT FILE: JOEY'S LIST

FULL NAME: Joseph Anthony Fatone, Jr.

NICKNAMES: Joey, Phat 1

BIRTHDAY: January 28, 1977

BIRTHPLACE: Brooklyn, New York

HAIR COLOR: Brown

EYE COLOR: Brown

PARENTS' NAMES: Phyllis and Joseph Fatone

BROTHER'S NAME: Stephen

SISTER'S NAME: Janine

HEIGHT: 6 feet

FAVORITE ACTOR: Robert DeNiro

FAVORITE ACTRESS: Sandra Bullock

FAVORITE MOVIE: Willy Wonka and the Chocolate Factory

FAVORITE DRINK: Soda

FAVORITE SALAD DRESSING: Italian

FAVORITE SPORT: Basketball (to watch, not to play)

FAVORITE SINGER: Frankie Lymon

FAVORITE FAMILY VACATION: The first time he went to Florida when he was eight years old

Joey is a huge movie buff. In fact, he and Lance will appear in a movie together called *On the Line*. It's a funny romance story, and in it Lance and Joey play best friends.

FIRST PET: A bird named Finchy

PET HE HAS NOW: A dog named Nikita

FAVORITE AUTHOR: Roald Dahl

WHAT MAKES HIM FEEL GOOD: Dancing

FAVORITE FOOD: Italian, especially pizza

FAVORITE CEREAL: Corn Pops, Count Chocula

FAVORITE CANDY: Big Red gum and Whatchamacallit chocolate bars

FAVORITE ICE-CREAM FLAVOR: Mint chocolate chip

FAVORITE COLOR: Purple

FAVORITE THING TO BUY: Anything with Superman on it

WORST HABIT: Being lazy

FIRST CONCERT: Boyz II Men

Joey likes to change his look — a lot! His hair has gone from brown to blond to red to brown again!

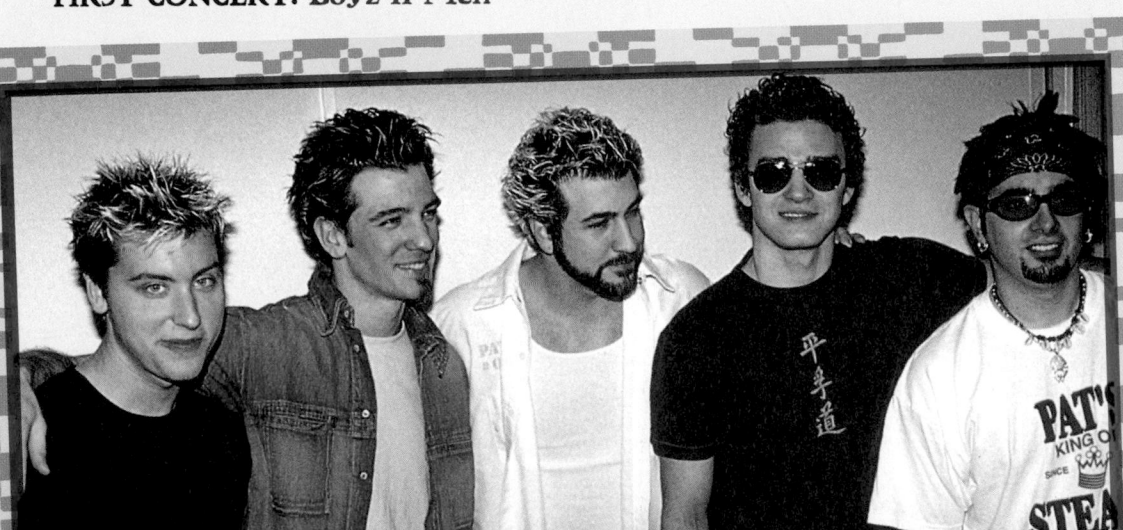

If you see Joey and you want to meet him, just walk up to him and be yourself!

CHAPTER 8

FACT FILE: LANCE AT A GLANCE

FULL NAME: James Lance Bass

NICKNAME: Scoop

BIRTHDAY: May 4, 1979

BIRTHPLACE: Laurel, Mississippi

HAIR COLOR: Blond

EYE COLOR: Green

PARENTS' NAMES: Diane and Jim Bass

SISTER'S NAME: Stacy

HEIGHT: 5 feet, 11 inches

FAVORITE ACTOR: Tom Hanks

FAVORITE ACTRESSES: Meg Ryan, Lucille Ball

FAVORITE MOVIE: *Clue*

FAVORITE SPORT: Football

FAVORITE SINGERS: Garth Brooks, Celine Dion

FIRST PET: A cocker spaniel named Goldie

PET HE HAS NOW: A cocker spaniel named Lexi

WHAT MAKES HIM FEEL GOOD: Going to the movies

FAVORITE FOOD: French toast

FAVORITE DRINK: Barq's Red Cream Soda

FAVORITE CANDY: Caramello bars

FAVORITE COLOR: Red

FAVORITE THING TO BUY: Gifts for his family

WORST HABIT: Forgetting things

FIRST CONCERT: Reba McEntire

Lance loved studying science and math in school.

16

Here's Lance hanging out with 98° guy Justin Jeffre. See, boy bands can play nicely together!

Lance is so happy with his own success that he wanted to help out other musicians. He started a company called Free-Lance Entertainment and one of the first singers he has helped launch is Meredith Edwards. She's not a pop singer like Lance, but a country music singer. Keep an eye out for her!

WHAT WERE THEY LIKE WHEN THEY WERE KIDS?

Part 2: Justin & Chris

If you stopped laughing about Joey, Lance, and JC, now's your turn to giggle at Justin and Chris from their school days.

Justin went to E.E. Jeter Elementary School in Millington, Tennessee. As you can see, his hair was a little flat back then. Justin has always had "issues" with his hair — he says the only time he ever got a spanking was when he tried to cut it himself!

Can you pick Justin out of this basketball team photo? He's #12 — top row, the second from the left.

Justin was voted "Mr. Jeter" at school. That doesn't mean he can play baseball like Derek Jeter, it means that he was very well liked by everyone.

Did you know that Chris played the trombone? In addition to singing in the choir, he was also in the school band. (In this photo, he's in the center.)

Justin has a collection of basketball trophies from his school days. Little did he know when he was young that he would get many more awards — but those would be for music, not sports.

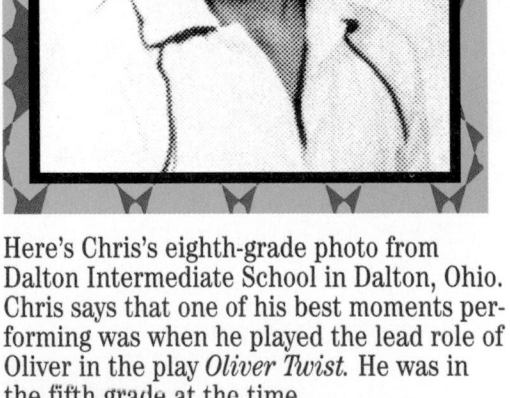

Here's Chris's eighth-grade photo from Dalton Intermediate School in Dalton, Ohio. Chris says that one of his best moments performing was when he played the lead role of Oliver in the play *Oliver Twist*. He was in the fifth grade at the time.

Justin isn't the only one who was into basketball as a kid. Chris is the first from the right (bottom row) on his school's team.

FACT FILE: ALL ABOUT JC

JC may be a big-time pop star, but he loves listening to jazz when he has a moment to himself.

FULL NAME: Joshua Scott Chasez

NICKNAME: JC

BIRTHDAY: August 8, 1976

BIRTHPLACE: Washington, D.C.

HAIR COLOR: Brown

EYE COLOR: Blue

PARENTS' NAMES: Karen and Roy Chasez

BROTHER'S NAME: Tyler

SISTER'S NAME: Heather

HEIGHT: 5 feet, 10 $\frac{1}{2}$ inches

FAVORITE ACTOR: Harrison Ford

FAVORITE ACTRESS: Meg Ryan

FAVORITE ANIMAL: Dog

FIRST PET: A dog named Grits

PET HE HAS NOW: A dog named Baron

FAVORITE AUTHOR: William Shakespeare

FAVORITE MOVIE: *Star Wars*

FAVORITE DRINK: Water

FAVORITE SPORT: Football

FAVORITE SINGERS: Sting, Seal

WHAT MAKES HIM FEEL GOOD: Sleeping

FAVORITE FOOD: Chinese

JC is full of energy onstage, but when he's offstage, he likes to sleep as much as he can.

JC went wild with the hair gel!

FAVORITE ICE-CREAM FLAVOR:
Mint chocolate chip

FAVORITE COLOR: Blue

GOOD LUCK CHARM: His lion necklace

BIGGEST FEAR: Needles

FIRST CONCERT: MC Hammer

CHAPTER 11

'N SYNC NOW!

'N Sync has done so many things, it's hard to keep track of them all. And they're not slowing down! They've actually taken on a lot of new projects. Joey, Lance, and Justin are doing some more acting. JC is writing music for other artists. Chris keeps busy with his clothing line called FuMan Skeeto. Look at what they've accomplished — who knows what these five will think up next?

Music Madness

The group's three albums, *'N Sync*, *No Strings Attached*, and *Celebrity*, flew off the shelves in no time at all. Whether they're singing "I Want You Back," "Bye Bye Bye," or "Pop," they've captured the hearts of fans all over the world. You might think that they would sit back and rest on their success, but JC, Joey, Lance, Chris, and Justin keep working harder and harder to make their fans happy. *Celebrity* is a CD that came from 'N Sync's heart because they wrote so much of it themselves. And they loved playing around in the recording studio by mixing all kinds of music — R&B, pop, electronica, country, and even dance music. "We just like to make what we think is good music into one album," says Chris. When they get creative, they certainly keep their fans on their toes!

Justin, Chris, and JC proudly accept their surfboard award at the Teen Choice Awards.

Justin is very close with his parents. In fact, his mother now has a business of her own called Just-In Time Entertainment. (It's named after her son, of course.) Like Lance's Free-Lance Entertainment, she helps to discover talented new singers.

You can always find 'N Sync on MTV's *Total Request Live* — so it makes sense that the guys have brought home many MTV Video Music Awards.

23

Movie Making

The guys have all talked about making a movie together. In fact, they even spoke with actor Tom Hanks about some of the ideas they had. Though Joey and Lance went after their dream of appearing on the silver screen in *On the Line*, all five guys appeared on the BIG screen. An IMAX movie called *'N Sync: Bigger Than Live*, which was released in March 2001, showcased the boys' tour show. Since IMAX movie screens are way more gigantic than a normal movie screen, you get a closer-than-front-row seat to their show. That means seeing everything from the details on their costumes to close-ups of Justin's fingers. (If you're curious, surf on to www.nsyncbiggerthanlive.com.)

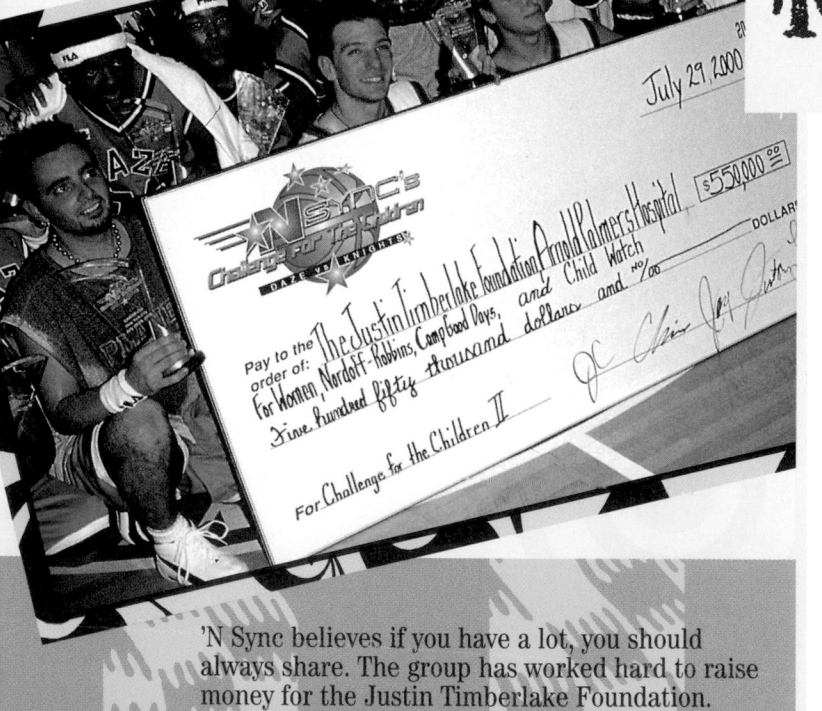

'N Sync believes if you have a lot, you should always share. The group has worked hard to raise money for the Justin Timberlake Foundation. Each year they organize a celebrity basketball game and the money goes to children's charities.

The Wonderful Justin of Oz?

Justin may be a TV star once again! If you love the story of the *Wizard of Oz*, don't you think you'd love it ten times more if Justin were in it? He may be! Justin was interested in playing the scarecrow who wanted a brain in this cool remake of the famous flick. The story is a little bit different this time around. Instead of taking place in Kansas, the story is set in Los Angeles. And instead of Dorothy being a girl who lives on a farm, Dorothy is a hip-hop music producer who finds herself in a whole new world after an earthquake! Keep an eye out for *The O.Z.* on Fox.

Surf over to www.nsync.com if you want to visit 'N Sync online. Or write them a letter and send it to: 'N Sync Fan Club, P.O. Box 5248, Bellingham, WA 98227